AAT Level 3

Advanced Synoptic

Practice Assessment

ADSY

Practice Assessment

By

Teresa Clarke FMAAT

This practice assessment has been designed and written to be as similar as possible to the real AAT Level 3 Advanced Synoptic ADSY exam. It includes a similar mark scheme so you can work out your percentage pass rate too.

Answers are shown on page 20 onwards.

A marks sheet is included at the back of this assessment for you to record your marks.

You need 70% to pass this exam.

NOTE: This practice assessment is for the first part of the advanced synoptic exam and does not include any spreadsheets tasks.

Time allowed = 2 hours 30 minutes

The assessment is made up of 6 tasks and each task is independent.

The whole assessment carries a total of 80 marks.

Minus signs or brackets are acceptable for negative numbers.

You may use a comma to denote thousands, but this is not required.

The assessment includes tasks from Advanced Bookkeeping, Final Accounts Preparation, Management Accounting: Costing and Professional Ethics.

Task 1: (15 marks)

This task is based on a workplace scenario separate from the rest of the assessment.

Niki is an accountant who works for a large accountancy practice. Harvey has recently joined the organisation as a trainee accountant and has made the following statements.

a) Identify whether the statements are true or false. (3 marks)

Statement	True	False
I only have a duty to apply my professional ethical principles once I become qualified.		✓
Professional ethical principles are based on the Code of Ethics which is a set of rules that every accountant must follow.	✓	

b) Identify whether the following actions are required by Harvey in his new job role. (2 marks)

Action	True	False
Comply with the rules and guidelines of the organisation.	✓	
Work unpaid overtime to ensure all work is completed within required timeframes.	✓	

c) Niki completes all her work to the best of her abilities, taking time to check her work for any errors. Which ONE of the following fundamental ethical principles is Niki complying with? (2 marks)

Professional competence and due care	✓
Confidentiality	
Objectivity	

d) Harvey has breached his fundamental ethical principle of confidentiality by disclosing confidential information to friends outside of his workplace. Which TWO of the following disciplinary actions could Harvey face? (2 marks)

Disciplinary action	
Disciplinary procedures may be taken against him by his employer.	✓
Disciplinary procedures may be taken against him by the AAT.	✓
Disciplinary procedures may be taken against him by the NCA.	

e) Niki has found a material error in the previous VAT return submitted by her finance director. Identify which ONE of the following actions Niki should take. (2 marks)

Action	
Advise HMRC of the error immediately.	
Ignore as she did not prepare the VAT return containing the error.	
Advise her finance director of the error immediately.	✓

f) The finance director has told Niki to ignore this error or face instant dismissal. Which one of the following threats is Niki facing to her fundamental ethical principles? (2 marks)

Threat	
Familiarity	
Intimidation	
Advocacy	

g) Niki has asked Harvey to complete some training in order that he may assist with the payroll for the organisation. Which ONE of the following fundamental ethical principles would Harvey be complying with by undertaking this training? (2 marks)

Fundamental ethical principle	
Professional behaviour	
Professional competence and due care	
Objectivity	

Task 2: (12 marks)

You are a trainee accountant for O & M Components Ltd. You complete a variety of tasks in your role. You report to your line manager on all aspects of your job role.

a) The following is an extract from an invoice which has been partially prepared. You have been asked to complete it. Enter the appropriate numbers in the boxes below. (1 mark)

Sub-total	£4,186.25
VAT	
Total	

b) You have noticed that another invoice has been posted with VAT at 30%. What effect will this have on the profit for the organisation? (1 mark)

No effect	
Profit will be higher than it should be.	
Profit will be lower than it should be.	

c) If the invoice remains unchanged, what effect will this have on the VAT payable to HMRC? (1 mark)

No effect	
More VAT will be payable to HMRC.	
Less VAT will be payable to HMRC.	

d) You discover that the senior finance director at O & M Components Ltd has been selling products as a substantially reduced price to his sister, disguising this as a substantial trade discount. (2 marks)

By applying the conceptual framework, complete the following sentences.

The senior finance director is facing a _____ *familiarity* _____

threat to his _____ *professional* *behaviour* _____
objectivity self interest

e) After discovery of this matter, what action should you take? (1 mark)

Report the matter to the NCA immediately.	
Report the matter to a senior colleague.	✓
Report the matter to the Police.	

f) The senior finance director asks you to keep quiet about the reduced selling prices and in return has offered you promotion to a more senior role with immediate effect. What threat are you facing to your fundamental ethical principles? (2 marks)

Familiarity threat	
Intimidation threat	
Self-interest threat	✓

g) Your line manager has asked you to reconstruct the sales ledger control account for O & M Components Ltd to calculate the discounts allowed for the month. You have been provided with the following information. Complete the ledger account below calculating the discounts allowed as the missing figure. (4 marks)

Opening balance of money owed by credit customers	£540,600
Closing balance of money owed by credit customers	£475,640
Receipts from credit customers	£670,500
Credit notes issued to credit customers	£ 6,500
Credit sales	£700,640
Irrecoverable debts	£ 12,300

Sales ledger control account

540600

Dr op. bal.	£	Dr	£
Closing balance 475640		BANK	670500
credit sales	700640	Credit note	6500
		opening bal	540600
		Irrec.	12300
			495640
	1241240	Discount allow	76300
			1212990
	1176250		1064940
	BANK		

Task 3: (13 marks)

This task is based on a scenario separate from the rest of the assessment.

You are working as an assistant accountant, reporting to Jo. Jo is a qualified accountant.

a) Today's date is 1 August 2021 and you have been provided with the following costing information.

The total material in stock on 1 July 2021 was 1200 Kg with a value of £3,600.

The following movements of stock took place during the month.

8 July   Receipt of 1400 Kg at a cost of £2.20 per Kg.

16 July   Receipt of 1500 Kg with a total cost of £3,775.

22 July   2200 Kg of raw material issued to production.

Complete the table below for the issue to production. (2 marks)

FIFO	£	5800
AVCO	£	5610

b) Complete the following sentence concerning the journal entries for closing inventory. (1 mark)

Closing inventory is **debited/credited** to the statement of financial position and **debited/credited** to the statement of profit or loss.

c) You have been provided with the value of the closing inventory using two different methods. Explain why these differ. (4 marks)

Closing inventory value using the marginal costing method.	£3,000
Closing inventory value using the absorption costing method.	£3,500

MARGINAL

PRIME +
VARIABLE

ABSORBTION

PRIME + V
+ F

d) Explain the effect on the profit of the business by using each of the methods. (2 marks)

1400   2.20   3080

1500   2.52   3775

2200   1200 3 = 3600
       1000 2.20 = 2200

1200 | 360

1400 | 300
2600 | 6 68
1500 | 2777
4100 | 10957
-2200 | 5800

1900 | 4657

e) You are told that the sales for the year were £780,000. The business has

a policy of using 30% mark-up to calculate the sales price.

Total purchases for the period were £700,000.

Opening inventory was valued at £25,000.

Calculate the value of the closing inventory. (4 marks)

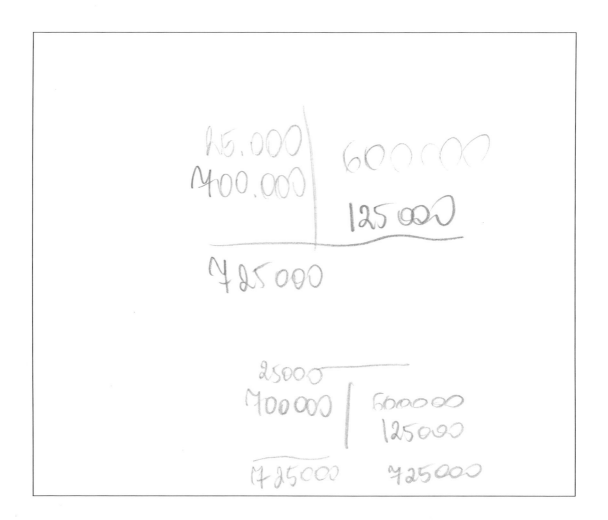

25.000
400.000
600000
125 000

725 000

25000
700 000   600000
               125000

725000   725000

780 000   130%.

60.
                              sales
                        Cos   600
                        Gross

Task 4: (15 marks)

This task is based on a scenario separate from the rest of the assessment. You are working as an accounts assistant for a small business. You are responsible for all invoicing and bookkeeping tasks, reporting to an external accountant for completion of accounts.

a) You have received a telephone call from the bank asking for the company accounts as a matter of urgency. You are aware that this is needed for an urgent loan request by the business, but you have not yet sent the information to the external accountant. The bank is requesting that you send the accounts directly to them by the end of the day. Failure to do this could mean that the loan is rejected, and jobs could be lost, including your own.

Describe a threat to your fundamental principles because of this request. (2 marks)

self intrest   to   prof. compeherce
intimidetion   to   →

b) Explain what action you should take as a result of this request. (2 marks)

c) Why do you, as an accounts assistant, have a responsibility to support sustainability? (1 mark)

d) You have received a request from the director of your company. The director has good business knowledge but limited accounting knowledge. The director has asked if you could explain the difference between a partnership and a limited company. You need to reply by email to your director and make sure that you include the following. (10 marks)

A brief description of a partnership,

A brief description of a partnership appropriation account,

A brief description of a limited company,

One key advantage of a partnership, and

One key advantage of a limited company.

Task 5: (12 marks)

a) You are working as a junior management accountant. You have been provided with the following budget and asked to flex this budget in order to compare the budget to the actual results. Complete the table below with the required information. Show adverse variances as negative numbers. (6 marks)

	Original budget 1,000 units	Flexed budget	Actual results 1,350 units	Variance
Sales £	50,000	67500	68,850	1350
Variable costs £	8,000	10800	11,286	-486
Fixed costs £	6,500	6500	6,305	195
Operating profit £	35,500	47925	51,259	-3334

b) Your manager has asked you to calculate the variances as a percentage of the budget. Using the results from the table above, complete the following boxes. Round your answers to two decimal places. (4 marks)

	Variance £	Percentage variance %
Sales	1350	
Variable costs	486	45
Fixed costs	185	
Operating profit	3334	

c) Identify whether each of the following costs are fixed or variable. (2 marks)

Cost per 1,000 units	Cost per 2,000 units	Cost per 5,000 units	Cost per 8,000 units	Fixed	Variable
£2,000	£4,000	£10,000	£16,000	✓	
£5,000	£5,000	£5,000	£5,000		✓

Task 6: (13 marks)

a) Record the following adjustments into the extract of the trial balance below. Not all cells require entries. Do not enter zeros in empty cells. (7 marks)

Closing inventory has been valued at £10,500

Irrecoverable debts of £300 need to be recorded

Discounts received of £60 need to be recorded

Motor expenses of £80 have been recorded as admin expenses

PLSA
dr/Purch

Account	Adjustment Dr	Adjustment Cr
Admin expenses		80
Closing inventory – statement of profit or loss		10500
Closing inventory – statement of financial position	10500	
Discounts received	60	
Irrecoverable debts	300	300
Motor expenses	80	
Purchases		
Purchases ledger control account		60
Sales		
Sales ledger control account		300

b) You have been provided with the following information about a partnership. The partners are Roxi, Mo and Ajay.

Net profit for the year   £210,000

You are told that the three partners each take a salary of £20,000 per year. The remaining profit is shared between the partners in the ratio of 3:2:1.

The partners took out the following drawings during the year:

Roxi £40,000   Mo £32,000   Ajay £28,000

Complete the current accounts below for the three partners, clearly showing the balance b/d. (6 marks)

Current accounts

Dr	Roxi £	Mo £	Ajay £	Cr	Roxi £	Mo £	Ajay £
Bal b/d		2,000		Bal b/d	1,400		7,000
Drawings	40000	32000	28000	Salary	20000	20000	20000
c/d	56400	36000	52000		75000	50000	25000
	96400	70000	24000		96400	70000	52000

Answers

Answers are shown in bold.

Workings and explanations are included to help you understand the answers and these are shown at the end of each task.

Task 1: (15 marks)

This task is based on a workplace scenario separate from the rest of the assessment.

Niki is an accountant who works for a large accountancy practice. Harvey has recently joined the organisation as a trainee accountant and has made the following statements.

a) Identify whether the statements are true or false. (3 marks)

Statement	True	False
I only have a duty to apply my professional ethical principles once I become qualified.		√
Professional ethical principles are based on the Code of Ethics which is a set of rules that every accountant must follow.		√

Explanation:
There is a duty for all accountants to apply professional ethics, regardless of whether they are qualified or not.
Professional ethics are based on a Code of Ethics which is a set of guidelines, not rules.

b) Identify whether the following actions are required by Harvey in his new job role. (2 marks)

Action	True	False
Comply with the rules and guidelines of the organisation.	√	
Work unpaid overtime to ensure all work is completed within required timeframes.		√

Explanation:

Rules and guidelines of the organisation must be followed to comply with Professional Behaviour.

He would not be expected to work unpaid.

c) Niki completes all her work to the best of her abilities, taking time to check her work for any errors. Which ONE of the following fundamental ethical principles is Niki complying with? (2 marks)

Professional competence and due care	√
Confidentiality	
Objectivity	

Explanation:

By taking time to check her work she is taking 'due care' in her work, so complying with professional competence and due care.

d) Harvey has breached his fundamental ethical principle of confidentiality by disclosing confidential information to friends outside of his workplace. Which TWO of the following disciplinary actions could Harvey face? (2 marks)

Disciplinary action	
Disciplinary procedures may be taken against him by his employer.	√
Disciplinary procedures may be taken against him by the AAT.	√
Disciplinary procedures may be taken against him by the NCA.	

Explanation:

He has breached his employment contract or company policy, so the employer could take disciplinary action, such as a verbal or written warning about his behaviour.

The AAT may take disciplinary action because he has breached his professional ethics.

It is not a matter for the NCA as they deal with serious crime, such as money laundering.

e) Niki has found a material error in the previous VAT return submitted by her finance director. Identify which ONE of the following actions Niki should take. (2 marks)

Action	
Advise HMRC of the error immediately.	
Ignore as she did not prepare the VAT return containing the error.	
Advise her finance director of the error immediately.	√

Explanation:

The first step would be to inform her finance director as he may not have been aware of the error.

f) The finance director has told Niki to ignore this error or face instant dismissal. Which one of the following threats is Niki facing to her fundamental ethical principles? (2 marks)

Threat	
Familiarity	
Intimidation	√
Advocacy	

Explanation:

Niki is being threatened with dismissal which is intimating her. Therefore, she faces an intimidation threat.

g) Niki has asked Harvey to complete some training in order that he may assist with the payroll for the organisation. Which ONE of the following fundamental ethical principles would Harvey be complying with by undertaking this training? (2 marks)

Fundamental ethical principle	
Professional behaviour	
Professional competence and due care	√
Objectivity	

Explanation:

Harvey will be improving his skills to carry out a new task. Therefore, he is becoming more competent in his role, so professional competence and due care.

Task 2: (12 marks)

You are a trainee accountant for O & M Components Ltd. You complete a variety of tasks in your role. You report to your line manager on all aspects of your job role.

a) The following is an extract from an invoice which has been partially prepared. You have been asked to complete it. Enter the appropriate numbers in the boxes below. (1 mark)

Sub-total	£4,186.25
VAT	**£837.25**
Total	**£5,023.50**

Workings:
4186.25 x 20% = 837.25. 4186.25 + 837.25 = 5023.50.

b) You have noticed that another invoice has been posted with VAT at 30%. What effect will this have on the profit for the organisation? (1 mark)

No effect	√
Profit will be higher than it should be.	
Profit will be lower than it should be.	

Explanation:
The VAT has been entered at 30% which means that 30% will be collected from the customer and paid over to HMRC. Therefore, there is no effect on the profit.

c) If the invoice remains unchanged, what effect will this have on the VAT payable to HMRC? (1 mark)

No effect	
More VAT will be payable to HMRC.	√
Less VAT will be payable to HMRC.	

Explanation:

The VAT will be charged at a higher rate to the customer so more will be paid to HMRC.

d) You discover that the senior finance director at O & M Components Ltd has been selling products as a substantially reduced price to his sister, disguising this as a substantial trade discount. (2 marks)

By applying the conceptual framework, complete the following sentences.

The senior finance director is facing a ___*familiarity*___

threat to his ___*objectivity*___ .

Explanation:

This is a familiarity threat because he is selling products cheaper to his sister and this is a threat to his objectivity because he is using bias. He is not treating her the same as other customers.

e) After discovery of this matter, what action should you take? (1 mark)

Report the matter to the NCA immediately.	
Report the matter to a senior colleague.	√
Report the matter to the Police.	

Explanation:

Your first step would be to tell a senior colleague to get their advice. The Police would not be an appropriate authority and the NCA deal with serious crime, such as money laundering.

f) The senior finance director asks you to keep quiet about the reduced selling prices and in return has offered you promotion to a more senior role with immediate effect. What threat are you facing to your fundamental ethical principles? (2 marks)

Familiarity threat	
Intimidation threat	
Self-interest threat	√

Explanation:

This is a self-interest threat because you will gain by keeping quiet. You have been offered promotion and this would be tempting.

g) Your line manager has asked you to reconstruct the sales ledger control account for O & M Components Ltd to calculate the discounts allowed for the month. You have been provided with the following information. Complete the ledger account below calculating the discounts allowed as the missing figure. (4 marks)

Opening balance of money owed by credit customers	£540,600
Closing balance of money owed by credit customers	£475,640
Receipts from credit customers	£670,500
Credit notes issued to credit customers	£ 6,500
Credit sales	£700,640
Irrecoverable debts	£ 12,300

Sales ledger control account

Dr	£	Dr	£
Bal b/d	540,600	Bank (receipts from customers)	670,500
Sales	700,640	Sales returns (credit notes)	6,500
		Irrecoverable debts (written off)	12,300
		Bal c/d	475,640
		Discounts allowed	76,300
	1,241,240		1,241,240
Bal b/d	475,640		

Explanation:

Always start by putting in the balance brought down. This is an asset account because it is money owed to the business. Assets are debits. The only other thing that will be entered on the debit side will be more sales on credit. All other entries are made on the credit side. Balance off the accounts by entered the total for the highest side and then the missing or balancing figure is the missing discounts allowed figure.

Task 3: (13 marks)

This task is based on a scenario separate from the rest of the assessment.

You are working as an assistant accountant, reporting to Jo. Jo is a qualified accountant.

a) Today's date is 1 August 2021 and you have been provided with the following costing information.

The total material in stock on 1 July 2021 was 1200 Kg with a value of £3,600.

The following movements of stock took place during the month.

8 July	Receipt of 1400 Kg at a cost of £2.20 per Kg.
16 July	Receipt of 1500 Kg with a total cost of £3,775.
22 July	2200 Kg of raw material issued to production.

Complete the table below for the issue to production. (2 marks)

FIFO	£5,800
AVCO	£5,610

Workings and explanation:

FIFO. The issue uses the oldest stock first (first in first out). 1200Kg of stock with a value of £3,600 was in stock at the beginning of the month, so we use that first. Then we need another 1000Kg of stock from the receipt of 8 July. 1000 x £2.20 = £2,200. £3,600 + £2,200 = £5,800.

AVCO. The issue uses the average cost of all stock held. We add up the quantity and add up the total value. 1200Kg + 1400Kg + 1500Kg = 4100Kg. £3,600 + £3,080 + £3,775 = £10,455. Divide the money by the units. £10,455 / 4100Kg = £2.55 per Kg. Multiply this by the quantity of the issue. £2.55 x 2200Kg = £5,610.

b) Complete the following sentence concerning the journal entries for closing inventory. (1 mark)

Closing inventory is ***debited*/credited** to the statement of financial position and **~~debited~~/*credited*** to the statement of profit or loss.

Explanation:

The best way to remember which statement is debited and which is credited is to remember that closing inventory is something the business owns right now. Therefore, this is an asset. Assets are debits. Assets are in the Statement of Financial Position. The credit entry will therefore be in the Statement of Profit or Loss.

c) You have been provided with the value of the closing inventory using two different methods. Explain why these differ. (4 marks)

Closing inventory value using the marginal costing method.	£3,000
Closing inventory value using the absorption costing method.	£3,500

Suggested answer: (note that your answer will not be exactly the same, but you make sure you understand the answer). Use an example to show your understanding if you think that will help.

The closing inventory using marginal costing includes the direct costs and the variable production costs.

The closing inventory using marginal costing includes the direct costs, the variable production costs, and some fixed production overheads.

For example:
Direct labour and direct materials are £10 per unit. Variable production costs are £5 per unit. So, the value of one unit of closing inventory using marginal costing would be £15 per unit.
If the fixed production overheads per unit are £12, then one unit of closing inventory using absorption costing would be £27 (£15 + £12 – the marginal cost plus the fixed production overheads).

Therefore, the closing inventory using absorption costing will have a higher value than the closing inventory using marginal costing.

d) Explain the effect on the profit of the business by using each of the methods. (2 marks)

Suggested answer: *(note that your answer will not be exactly the same, but you make sure you understand the answer). Use an example to show your understanding if you think that will help.*

The profit of the business will be lower with marginal costing and higher with absorption costing. This is because the cost of sales will be lower with absorption costing and higher with marginal costing.

Example:
Marginal costing
Sales   £100
Opening inventory   £10
Purchases   £50
Closing inventory   (£15)   £ 45
Gross profit   £ 55

Absorption costing
Sales   £100
Opening inventory   £10
Purchases   £50
Closing inventory   (£20)   £ 40
Gross profit   £ 60

Note: The marker will be looking for understanding so examples can be really useful.

---

e) You are told that the sales for the year were £780,000. The business has a policy of using 30% mark-up to calculate the sales price.

Total purchases for the period were £700,000.

Opening inventory was valued at £25,000.

Calculate the value of the closing inventory. (4 marks)

Mark-up
Cost of sales = 100%
Mark-up = 30%
Sales = £130%

Sales = £780,000 (130%)
Mark-up = £180,000 (30%)
Cost of sales = £600,000 (100%)

Cost of sales = Opening Inventory + Purchases – Closing Inventory
£600,000 = £25,000 + £700,000 - ?
£600,000 = £725,000 - ?
£725,000 - £600,000 = £125,000
Closing inventory = £125,000

Check: 25,000 + 700,000 – 125,000 = 600,000

Note: You can use any method you wish, so long as you get to the correct answer.

Task 4: (15 marks)

This task is based on a scenario separate from the rest of the assessment. You are working as an accounts assistant for a small business. You are responsible for all invoicing and bookkeeping tasks, reporting to an external accountant for completion of accounts.

a) You have received a telephone call from the bank asking for the company accounts as a matter of urgency. You are aware that this is needed for an urgent loan request by the business, but you have not yet sent the information to the external accountant. The bank is requesting that you send the accounts directly to them by the end of the day. Failure to do this could mean that the loan is rejected, and jobs could be lost, including your own.

Describe a threat to your fundamental principles because of this request. (2 marks)

Note: The question says describe, so a few words are not enough to gain full marks. Sometimes there are alternative answers, so make sure you describe what you believe is the correct answer as marks can be given for well explained alternative answers.

This is a <u>self-interest threat</u> to your professional competence and due care. This is because you have been asked to do something that you are not competent to do, but if you don't do it, you could lose your job.

An alternative answer could be: This is an <u>intimidation</u> threat to your professional competence and due care. This is because you feel pressurised into doing something that you are not competent to do, and failure to do it could mean that lots of people lose their jobs, including you..

b) Explain what action you should take as a result of this request. (2 marks)

> *Suggested answer:*
> *Note: There could be several acceptable answers for this question, so make sure you explain your action fully.*
>
> *Contact my line manager immediately to discuss what to do next.*
> *Or*
> *Contact the external accountant for their advice.*
> *Or*
> *Contact the AAT or other professional body for advice.*
> *Or*
> *Advise the bank that you will not be able to fulfil the request but will contact your manager to ask them to respond directly.*

c) Why do you, as an accounts assistant, have a responsibility to support sustainability? (1 mark)

> *Suggested answer:*
> **All accountants have a responsibility to promote sustainable development to meet the needs of today without compromising the ability of future generations to meet their needs.**
> **Or**
> **All accountants have a responsibility to support sustainability as it is in the public interest.**

d) You have received a request from the director of your company. The director has good business knowledge but limited accounting knowledge. The director has asked if you could explain the difference between a partnership and a limited company. You need to reply by email to your director and make sure that you include the following. (10 marks)

A brief description of a partnership,

A brief description of a partnership appropriation account,

A brief description of a limited company,

One key advantage of a partnership, and

One key advantage of a limited company.

Note: The task does not require you to give all information about partnerships and limited companies, so your answers will be different to mine. You are required to give a brief description, so just write as many details as you can think of. The marker is looking for a general understanding.

Dear Sir

Further to your request for information about partnerships and limited companies, I will explain these below.

A partnership is two or more people coming together in business with a view to make profit. They work together within the terms of their partnership agreement. The partnership agreement is set up at the start of the partnership to agree terms, such as job roles, capital introduced, times worked, holidays, drawings to be taken, profit share and more. At the end of the accounting period, usually a year, the statement of profit or loss and the statement of financial position are drawn up. Each partner is responsible for his own tax. The partnership prepares a partnership tax return, and each partner completes their own individual self-assessment tax return. They are essentially treated as two or more sole traders working together. If the business should fail, the partners would be responsible for any debts so their personal assets could be at risk. It is relatively cheap to set up a partnership. The net profit is shared between the partners under the terms of the partnership agreement, and this is drawn up as a Partnership Appropriation Account, which is shown at the bottom of the statement of profit and loss and shows the distribution of that profit. It includes the net profit, the salaries, any interest on capital and the profit share for the partners.

A limited company is a separate legal entity which means that it is owned by the shareholders and run by the directors. The limited company employs the directors to run the company and they are paid salaries. The shareholders can receive dividends from the profit of the company. The limited company must have a separate bank account and all money kept separate from the owners of the business. The company must be registered with Companies House and the accounts must be sent to Companies House at the end of the accounting period. These accounts are available for public view. It is expensive to set up and run a company as statutory accounts are required which must comply with IAS1. If the company should fail, the shareholders are not responsible for the debts as they have limited liability which means that any debts can only be recovered from the company, so any private assets are safe. Companies pay corporation tax.

One advantage of running the business as a partnership is that the accounts are private to the business and the partners. It is also cheap to set up.

One advantage of running the business as a limited company is that it has limited liability meaning that the shareholders are not responsible for any debts of the business.

If I can be of any more help, please let me know.

Kind regards,

Accounts assistant

Task 5: (12 marks)

a) You are working as a junior management accountant. You have been provided with the following budget and asked to flex this budget in order to compare the budget to the actual results. Complete the table below with the required information. Show adverse variances as negative numbers. (6 marks)

	Original budget 1,000 units	Flexed budget **1,350 units**	Actual results 1,350 units	Variance
Sales £	50,000	**67,500**	68,850	**1,350**
Variable costs £	8,000	**10,800**	11,286	**(486)**
Fixed costs £	6,500	**6,500**	6,305	**195**
Operating profit £	35,500	**50,200**	51,259	**1,059**

Workings and explanation:

There are different ways to calculate the flexed budget, but I would suggest the following.

Sales total divided by original budget quantity, multiplied by flexed budget quantity.

50,000 / 1,000 = 5   5 x 1,350 = 67,500

You can use the same process for the variable costs.

Fixed costs are fixed, so the revised, flexed budget will have the same fixed costs.

The profit is the sales, less the variable and fixed costs.

67,500 – 10,800 – 6,500 = 50,200

Tip: Don't look at the actual figures until you have completed the flexed budget.

The variance is the difference between the flexed budget and the actual figures. If the actual sales are higher than the flexed sales budget, this is a favourable variance, so a positive number. If the actual sales are lower than the flexed sales budget, this is an adverse variance, so a negative number. If the actual costs are less than the flexed budget, then this is a favourable variance, so a positive number. If the actual costs are higher than the flexed budget, this is an adverse variance, so a negative number.

b) Your manager has asked you to calculate the variances as a percentage of the budget. Using the results from the table above, complete the following boxes. Round your answers to two decimal places. (4 marks)

	Variance £	Percentage variance %
Sales	1,350	2.00
Variable costs	(486)	4.50
Fixed costs	195	3.00
Operating profit	1,059	2.11

Workings:

(1,350 / 67,500) x 100 = 2%

Variance divided by budgeted sales, multiplied by 100 gives the variance as a percentage.

The same method is used for the variable costs, fixed costs and operating profit.

(486 / 10,800) x 100 = 4.5%

(195 / 6,500) x 100 = 3%

(1,059 / 50,200) x 100 = 2.11% (rounded to 2 decimal places)

c) Identify whether each of the following costs are fixed or variable. (2 marks)

Cost per 1,000 units	Cost per 2,000 units	Cost per 5,000 units	Cost per 8,000 units	Fixed	Variable
£2,000	£4,000	£10,000	£16,000		√
£5,000	£5,000	£5,000	£5,000	√	

Explanation:

The first is a variable cost because variable cost varies per unit produced.

£2,000 divided by 1,000 units = £2 per unit

£4,000 divided by 2,000 units = £2 per unit

£10,000 divided by 5,000 units = £2 per unit

£16,000 divided by 8,000 units = £2 per unit

The second is a fixed cost because the cost remains the same and does not change with the amount of units produced, such as the rent of the building.

Task 6: (13 marks)

a) Record the following adjustments into the extract of the trial balance below. Not all cells require entries. Do not enter zeros in empty cells.
(7 marks)

Closing inventory has been valued at £10,500

Irrecoverable debts of £300 need to be recorded

Discounts received of £60 need to be recorded

Motor expenses of £80 have been recorded as admin expenses

Account	Adjustments Dr	Adjustments Cr
Admin expenses		80
Closing inventory – statement of profit or loss		10,500
Closing inventory – statement of financial position	10,500	
Discounts received		60
Irrecoverable debts	300	
Motor expenses	80	
Purchases		
Purchases ledger control account	60	
Sales		
Sales ledger control account		300

Explanation:

Remember to use DEAD CLIC for this type of question.

Motor expenses have been recorded as admin expenses, so these need to be taken out of the admin expenses and added to the motor expenses. Expenses are a debit, so we credit out of the admin expenses and debit to the motor expenses.

Irrecoverable debts is money that the business will not receive from the customer so this is 'written off' in the accounts. This costs the business money so this is an expense to the business. Expenses are debits. We debit the irrecoverable debts account and credit the sales ledger control account as this money is no longer receivable.

Discounts received are received by the business, so these are a form of income. Income is a credit. We credit the discounts received account and debit the purchase ledger control account because the discounts received reduce the amount we owe to the suppliers.

Closing inventory is an asset to the business as it is owned by the business. Assets are debits and assets are entered into the Statement of Financial Position. This is debited to the SOFP and credited to the Statement of Profit or Loss.

b) You have been provided with the following information about a partnership. The partners are Roxi, Mo and Ajay.

Net profit for the year £210,000

You are told that the three partners each take a salary of £20,000 per year. The remaining profit is shared between the partners in the ratio of 3:2:1.

The partners took out the following drawings during the year:

Roxi £40,000   Mo £32,000   Ajay £28,000

Complete the current accounts below for the three partners, clearly showing the balance b/d. (6 marks)

Current accounts

Dr	Roxi £	Mo £	Ajay £	Cr	Roxi £	Mo £	Ajay £
Bal b/d		2,000		Bal b/d	1,400		7,000
Drawings	40,000	32,000	28,000	Salary	20,000	20,000	20,000
				Profit share	75,000	50,000	25,000
Bal c/d	56,400	36,000	24,000				
	96,400	70,000	52,000		96,400	70,000	52,000
				Bal b/d	56,400	36,000	24,000

Explanation:
The profit is £210,000, the salaries total £60,000, so the residual profit for distribution is £150,000. This is shared 3:2:1.
£150,000 divided by 6 and multiplied by 3 is £75,000.
£150,000 / 6 and then multiplied by 2 = £50,000.
£150,000 / 6 x 1 = £25,000.
The current accounts show the money that is owed to the partners by the business and from the partners to the business. Money owed to the partners, such as salaries and profit shares are credited to the current accounts because these are owed to the partners. Money owed by the business is a liability and liabilities are credits. Money owed by the partners to the business, such as drawings or interest on drawings are debited to the current accounts because these are owed by the partners to the business. Money owed by the partners to the business are assets and assets are debits.
Enter all the figures into the current accounts, balance the highest side and put the same number on the opposite side. The balancing figure is the balance the

carry down or bal c/d. This is brought down on the opposite side as the bal b/d.

Note: If the balance brought down is on the credit side, the business owes the partner money. If the balance brought down is on the debit side, the partner owes the business money.

Marks sheet:

Task	Available marks	Your marks – first attempt	Your marks – second attempt	Notes
1a	3			
1b	2			
1c	2			
1d	2			
1e	2			
1f	2			
1g	2			
2a	1			
2b	1			
2c	1			
2d	2			
2e	1			
2f	2			
2g	4			
3a	2			
3b	1			
3c	4			
3d	2			
3e	4			
4a	2			
4b	2			
4c	1			
4d	10			
5a	6			
5b	4			
5c	2			
6a	7			
6b	6			
Total	80			

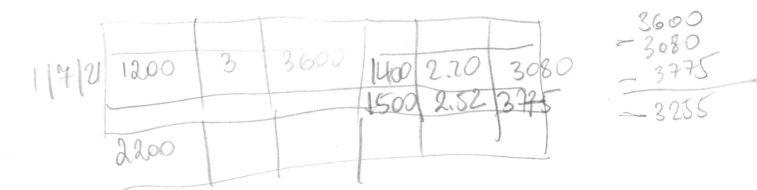

1|7|2|	1200	3	3600	1400	2.20	3080
				1500	2.52	3775
2200						

3600
- 3080
- 3775
- 3255